Zoom in on the
STATUE OF LIBERTY

ZOOM in
on American
Symbols

Cecelia H. Brannon

Enslow Publishing
101 W. 23rd Street
Suite 240
New York, NY 10011
USA

enslow.com

WORDS TO KNOW

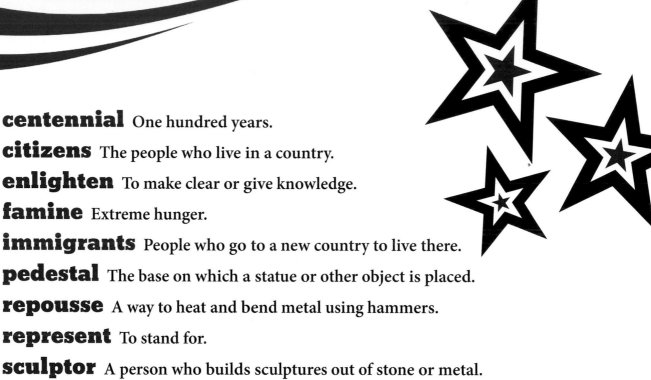

centennial One hundred years.

citizens The people who live in a country.

enlighten To make clear or give knowledge.

famine Extreme hunger.

immigrants People who go to a new country to live there.

pedestal The base on which a statue or other object is placed.

repousse A way to heat and bend metal using hammers.

represent To stand for.

sculptor A person who builds sculptures out of stone or metal.

symbol A thing that stands in for or represents something else.

CONTENTS

The Birth of the Statue

The Statue of Liberty is a famous American symbol. With her arm held high, she stands on Liberty Island in New York Harbor, overlooking the United States and her citizens. The statue has stood for more than one hundred years as a sign of hope to Americans and immigrants looking for a better life.

A Symbolic Gift

The Statue of Liberty was given to the United States by France for its centennial, or one hundredth birthday, in 1876. Her full name is Liberty Enlightening the World, and she represents freedom.

The idea for Lady Liberty, as the statue is known, began in 1865. It was the end of the

American Civil War, and a Frenchman named Edouard de Laboulaye wanted to mark the end of slavery and the freedom of all people. At the time, France was under the rule of Napoleon III, who was a cruel and unfair leader. Laboulaye wanted freedom in France like citizens of the United States had.

Working Together

One night, Laboulaye was talking with his friends about

Visiting the Statue

The Statue of Liberty can only be reached by ferry. Private boats cannot dock there, and there are no bridges or landing pads on the islands for vehicles or aircraft.

making something to represent American freedom. One of his friends was sculptor Frederic Auguste Bartholdi. Together, the men began designing the statue that would one day become Lady Liberty.

Laboulaye and Bartholdi wanted the statue to represent the freedom and liberty of the American people—the freedom that they hoped to one day have in France. So, they designed the statue after Libertas, the Roman goddess of liberty. She would wear a crown on her head and robes on her body, while holding a torch high, another symbol for liberty.

Frederic Auguste Bartholdi

Building Lady Liberty

Not all Americans wanted the gift that the French were offering. Many thought it would be expensive, as well as ugly. It took nearly ten years to build the statue because the project kept running out of money. It was finally agreed that France would build the statue and the United States would build the pedestal.

Bartholdi (*second from right*) and a group of men work on the statue's left hand.

Copper Creation

Bartholdi wanted to create the statue out of copper, so that it would shine in the sun. He used a method called repousse to create the statue. Workers heated the copper over and over again and used hammers to shape it. It is said that nearly six hundred different kinds of hammers were used to create the statue.

The outside would be a beautiful woman made

How Big Is Lady Liberty?

The Statue of Liberty is 305 feet (93 meters) tall from ground to crown, and 151 feet (46 meters) tall from head to toe. She weighs 204 metric tons and is made of the same amount of copper as thirty million pennies!

of shining copper. But what about the inside? For this, Laboulaye had help from Gustav Eiffel, another famous sculptor friend. Eiffel, whose famous tower has become a symbol for Paris, helped to create an iron frame for the inside of the statue. This frame has many stairs and levels and was built along with the statue itself, as the workers needed to get higher and higher as the statue grew.

A Home for the Statue

Laboulaye had to decide where to put such a large statue. When he arrived in New York City in 1874, he discovered an unused piece of land in the harbor called Bedloe's Island. It became the site for France's gift to America.

Liberty and Ellis Islands

The Statue of Liberty is most well known for welcoming immigrants into the United States. During the early 1900s, thousands of immigrants were escaping war and famine in Europe to come to America and begin new lives. Many crossed the ocean on steamships, and their journey could sometimes take two or three months!

Immigrants from Europe crowd the deck of a ship on its way to Ellis Island in 1906.

The American Immigrant Wall of Honor

The American Immigrant Wall of Honor is an exhibit of names of people who passed through Ellis Island to enter the United States. It is located on Ellis Island. To date, some 700,000 names are written on the wall.

First Sight in America

When they arrived in New York, the first thing many immigrants saw was the Statue of Liberty, welcoming them to their new country. Next to Liberty Island (as it was renamed in 1956), is another island that wasn't very well used. So, the United States government created an immigration center on Ellis Island, where immigrants were interviewed and given a medical exam. If they were

Immigrants at Ellis Island wait to take tests to see if they can stay in the United States.

healthy and promised to make good citizens, they were let into the United States. If they were not, they were sent back to their old country.

Hard Times

In 1916, during World War I, German soldiers attacked the Statue of Liberty, damaging the arm and torch. Until then, visitors were allowed to climb into the torch. Since the attack, however, visitors can only climb into the pedestal or the crown.

In 2012, Hurricane Sandy damaged both Liberty and Ellis Islands. They were closed for nearly a year while repairs were made. The Statue of Liberty reopened on July 4, 2013.

A Timeless Symbol

The statue's copper skin and dress, now green thanks to a chemical reaction that occurs when copper reacts with salt water, is a true symbol of the United States. The seven points on the crown represent the seven oceans and seven continents on Earth. The sandals that Lady Liberty wears on her feet represent the freedom of the common man, and the broken chains on which she stands represent the freedom that all Americans share.

Fourth of July fireworks are held in New York Harbor near Lady Liberty.

Calling the Huddled Masses

On the pedestal of the statue is a bronze plaque with a poem by Emma Lazarus, written while the statue was still being built. The poem ends with these famous welcoming lines:

Give me your tired, your poor,
Your huddled masses yearning
to breathe free,
The wretched refuse of your
teeming shore.
Send these, the homeless,
tempest-tost to me,
I lift my lamp beside the
golden door!

Freedom Forever!

Today, nearly four million people visit the statue each year, from every corner of the world. With her torch held high and her crown pointing to the sky, Lady Liberty is a timeless symbol for freedom. Her strength has helped bring the country together during hard times and reminds us that no matter what happens, Americans can look to the Statue of Liberty to remind us that we are free.

ACTIVITY
WHERE DID YOU COME FROM?

Many immigrants made their way through Ellis Island to enter the United States. Do you know where your family is from?

1. Ask your parents, grandparents, or other adults in your family if they know your family's background. Maybe they even know if your ancestors came through Ellis Island! Write down any information or stories your family members tell you.

2. If you are able to find out which countries your family comes from, see if you can find the place(s) on a map or globe.

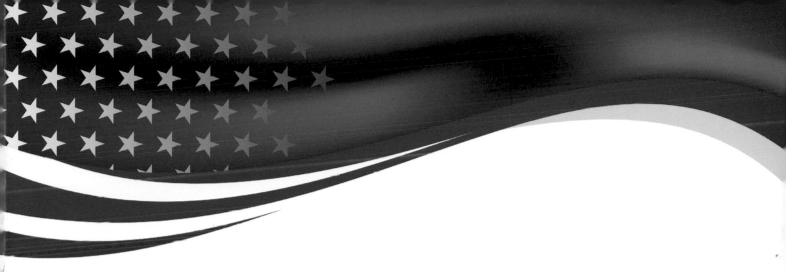

3. If you family doesn't know where your ancestors came from, there are many places online, and in museums and libraries, where you can find that information.

4. Try making a family tree. Start with yourself, then your parents, and see how far back you can trace your roots.

LEARN MORE

Books

Demuth, Patricia Brennan. *What Was Ellis Island?* New York, NY: Grosset & Dunlap, 2014.

Glaser, Linda. *Emma's Poem: The Voice of the Statue of Liberty*. New York, NY: HMH Books for Young Readers, 2013.

Holub, Joan. *What Is the Statue of Liberty?* New York, NY: Grosset & Dunlap, 2014.

Websites

National Park Service: Statue of Liberty
www.nps.gov/stli/learn/kidsyouth/index.htm
Learn more about Liberty Island.

The Statue of Liberty-Ellis Island Foundation
www.libertyellisfoundation.org
The official site of the Ellis Island Immigration Museum.

Statue of Liberty Tickets
www.statueoflibertytickets.com/Statue-Of-Liberty
Find information on visiting the Statue of Liberty.

INDEX

Published in 2017 by Enslow Publishing, LLC.
101 W. 23rd Street, Suite 240, New York, NY 10011

Copyright © 2017 by Enslow Publishing, LLC.

Library of Congress Cataloging-in-Publication Data
Names: Brannon, Cecelia H., author.
Title: Zoom in on the Statue of Liberty / Cecelia H. Brannon.
Description: New York, NY : Enslow Publishing, 2017. | Series: Zoom in on American symbols | Includes bibliographical references and index. | Audience: Grades K–3. | Audience: 7–up.
Identifiers: LCCN 2016021423 | ISBN 9780766084520 (library bound) | ISBN 9780766084506 (pbk.) | ISBN 9780766084513 (6-pack)
Subjects: LCSH: Statue of Liberty (New York, N.Y.)—Juvenile literature. | New York (N.Y.)—Buildings, structures, etc.—Juvenile literature.
Classification: LCC F128.64.L6 B74 2016 | DDC 974.7—dc23
LC record available at https://lccn.loc.gov/2016021423

Printed in China

To Our Readers: We have done our best to make sure all website addresses in this book were active and appropriate when we went to press. However, the author and the publisher have no control over and assume no liability for the material available on those websites or on any websites they may link to. Any comments or suggestions can be sent by e-mail to customerservice@enslow.com.

Photos Credits: Cover, p. 1 Timothy Clary/AFP/Getty Images; cover, p. 1 (background flag) Stillfx/Shutterstock.com; p. 5 AR Pictures/Shutterstock.com; p. 7 Mansell/The LIFE Picture Collection/Getty Images; p. 9 Library of Congress/Corbis Historical/Getty Images; p. 13 Bettmann/Getty Images; p. 15 Popperfoto/Getty Images; p. 17 From The New York Public Library; p. 19 Jeff Hunter/Photographer's Choice/Getty Images; p. 20 melanzane1013/Wikimedia Commons/File: Emma Lazarus plaque.jpg/CC BY-SA 2.0; interior pages graphic elements amtitus/DigitalVision Vectors/Getty Images (flag page borders), funnybank/DigitalVision Vectors/Getty Images (flag in circle), statue and skyline drmakkoy/DigitalVision Vectors/Getty Images.